I0813834

CHEERS FOR CAREERS!

I WANT TO BE AN AUTO MECHANIC

by Julie Murray

Cody Koala

An Imprint of Pop!
popbooksonline.com

Hello! My name is Cody Koala

This book is filled with videos, puzzles, games, and more! Scan the QR codes* while you read, or visit the website below to make this book pop.

popbooksonline.com/mechanic

*Scanning QR codes requires a web-enabled smart device with a QR code reader app and a camera.

abdobooks.com

Published by Pop!, a division of ABDO, PO Box 398166, Minneapolis, Minnesota 55439.

Printed in the United States of America, North Mankato, Minnesota.

052024
082024

Cover Photo: Shutterstock Images
Interior Photos: Getty Images, Shutterstock Images
Editor: Elizabeth Andrews and Grace Hansen
Series Designer: Colleen McLaren

Library of Congress Control Number: 2023947427

Publisher's Cataloging-in-Publication Data
Names: Murray, Julie, author.
Title: I want to be a auto mechanic / by Julie Murray
Description: Minneapolis, Minnesota : Pop!, 2025 | Series: Cheers for careers! | Includes online resources and index
Identifiers: ISBN 9781098246082 (lib. bdg.) | ISBN 9781098246648 (ebook)
Subjects: LCSH: Mechanics (Persons)--Juvenile literature. | Automobile mechanics--Juvenile literature. | Mechanic arts--Juvenile literature. | Servicing trades--Juvenile literature. | Occupations--Juvenile literature.
Classification: DDC 621.8--dc23

Table of Contents

Chapter 1
Working with Cars 4

Chapter 2
Skills Needed 6

Chapter 3
How to Become
an Auto Mechanic 12

Chapter 4
Different Jobs 18

Making Connections 22
Glossary 23
Index 24
Online Resources 24

Chapter 1

Working with Cars

Auto mechanics are also called auto technicians. They make repairs on vehicles and keep vehicles running well.

There are more than 230,000 auto mechanic businesses in the United States.
Watch a video here!

Chapter 2

Skills Needed

Auto mechanics work with customers. They need to explain the problems with a customer's vehicle. Then they have to present their plan to repair the vehicle.

Learn more here!

Auto mechanics should also have good problem-solving skills. They need to find the problem with a vehicle and know how to fix it.

Auto mechanics use computer programs to help find problems with a vehicle.

Auto mechanics perform tasks with their hands and work with many different tools. They need to have good **hand-eye coordination**.

ball-peen hammer
wrench
pry bar
pliers
wheel wrench
allen wrench
jack stand
tire gauge
ratchet and sockets

Chapter 3

How to Become an Auto Mechanic

Community and **technical colleges** offer auto mechanic training programs. These usually take one to two years to complete.

Explore links here!

Hands-on experience is important for auto mechanics too. This can be done through

an **apprenticeship**. This provides a good base for the career.

Most employers require that their auto mechanics are **certified**. This means that there is **official** proof that a person has been trained in areas such as engine and brake repair.

It can take two to four years to become a certified auto mechanic.

Chapter 4

Different Jobs

Most auto mechanics work for car dealerships or repair businesses. Some companies offer training programs. These may be geared toward specific vehicles.

Auto mechanics are in high demand in the United States.

Complete an activity here!

Some auto mechanics work on engine repair. Others may work on **electrical systems**. Whatever area one works, being an auto mechanic is a rewarding career!

Making Connections

Text-to-Self

Auto mechanics work on cars. What kind of car do you like best? Why?

Text-to-Text

Have you ever read another book about auto mechanics or cars? If so, what did you learn?

Text-to-World

There is a big need for auto mechanics in the United States. Why do you think this job is so important?

Glossary

apprenticeship – an arrangement in which someone learns a trade under an expert.

certified – having or verified by a certificate.

electrical system – a group of vehicle parts including the battery, starter, lights, and various other controls.

hand-eye coordination – the way that one's hands and sight work together to do things that require speed and accuracy.

official – approved by an authority.

technical college – a school that educates and prepares students for a specific trade or career.

Index

apprenticeship, 15

customers, 6

engine, 17, 21

jobs, 18

repair, 4, 6, 17, 18, 21

school, 12

skills, 9, 10

tools, 10

training, 12, 17, 18

vehicles, 4, 6, 9, 18

Online Resources

popbooksonline.com

Thanks for reading this Cody Koala book!

This book is filled with videos, puzzles, games, and more! Scan the QR codes* while you read, or visit the website below to make this book pop.

popbooksonline.com/mechanic

*Scanning QR codes requires a web-enabled smart device with a QR code reader app and a camera.